WHY DO I
WASH MY HANDS?

BookLife
PUBLISHING

©2021
BookLife Publishing Ltd.
King's Lynn
Norfolk PE30 4LS

A catalogue record for this book is available from the British Library.

ISBN: 978-1-83927-694-1

Written by:
Madeline Tyler

Edited by:
John Wood

Designed by:
Danielle Rippengill

Image Credits

All images are courtesy of Shutterstock.com, unless otherwise specified. With thanks to Getty Images, Thinkstock Photo and iStockphoto. Front Cover & 1 – jehsomwang, Nadzin, Dmitry Natashin. Images used on every page – Nadzin, Dmitry Natashin. Hands – jehsomwang. 5 – Iconic Bestiary. 7 – Finevector. 8&9 – svtdesign. 10 – Top Vector Studio, BlueRingMedia. 11 – Iconic Bestiary. 13 – Anna_leni. 14&15 – Iconic Bestiary. 15 – naulicreative. 18 – Anatolir. 19 – Mascha Tace. 20–23 – Iconic Bestiary.

CONTENTS

Words that look like **this** can be found in the glossary on page 24.

Helping Hands

We use our hands to touch things, push things, pull things and carry things. How many different things do you touch in a day?

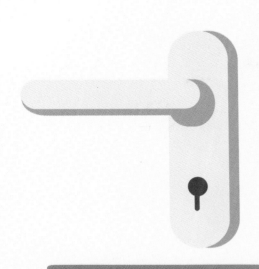

We open doors.

We play with toys.

We use tablets.

We eat lunch.

Are Your Hands Clean?

Look at your hands. Are they clean? Can you see any marks or bits of dirt on them?

Even when your hands look clean, there might be things on them that you can't see.

Think about all of the things you've touched today.
Were all of those things clean?

When we touch dirty things, it can make our hands dirty too.

Germs

Germs are tiny things that are around us all. Most germs do not hurt us, but some germs can make us ill if they get into our bodies.

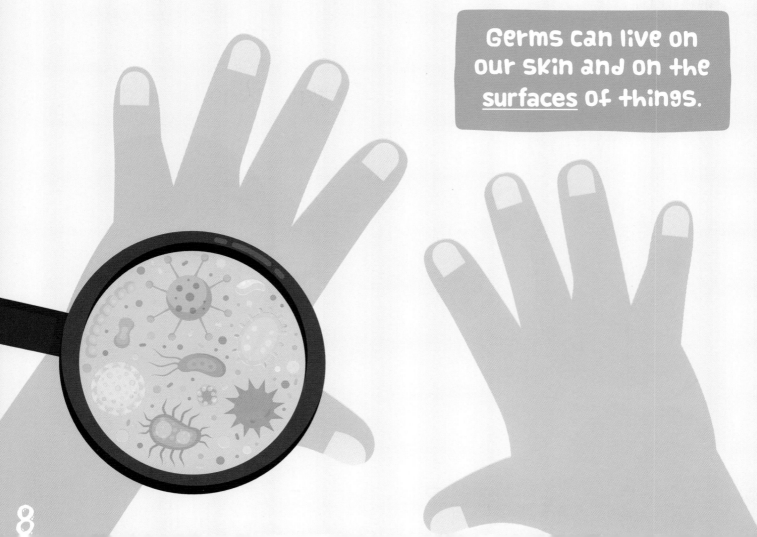

Germs can live on our skin and on the **surfaces** of things.

8

When you touch things, your hands can spread germs from one thing to another. If somebody is ill, the germs they pass on could cause other people to become ill.

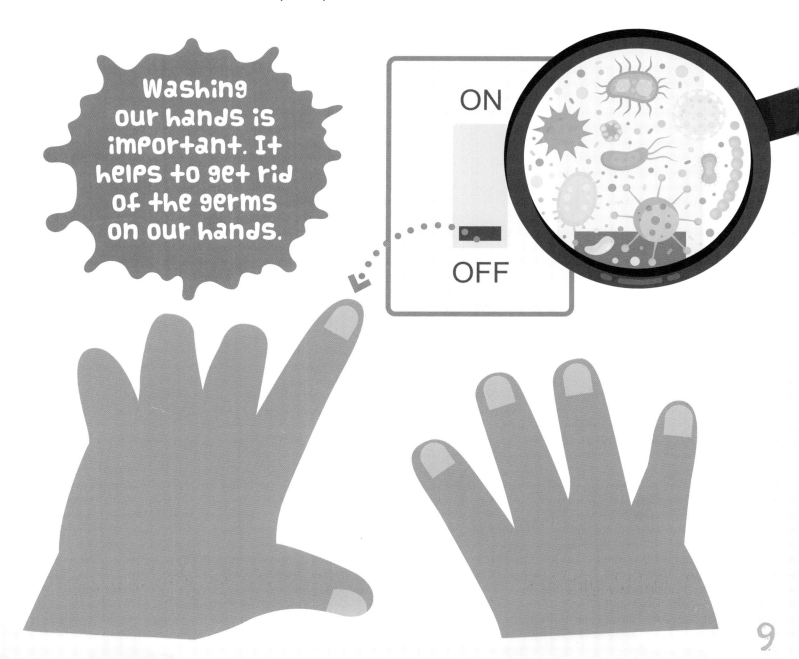

Washing our hands is important. It helps to get rid of the germs on our hands.

ON

OFF

Coughs

and Colds

When you have a cold or feel sick, it is probably because some germs have got inside your body.

You might have breathed them in or touched your face or your food with dirty hands.

Germs can be spread by coughing, sneezing and touching things. If you are ill, it is easy to spread this illness to someone else, even if you don't mean to.

Why Washing Works

Even if you think your hands are clean, or you don't feel unwell, it is very important to wash your hands many times throughout the day.

Washing with soap kills all the germs you cannot see.

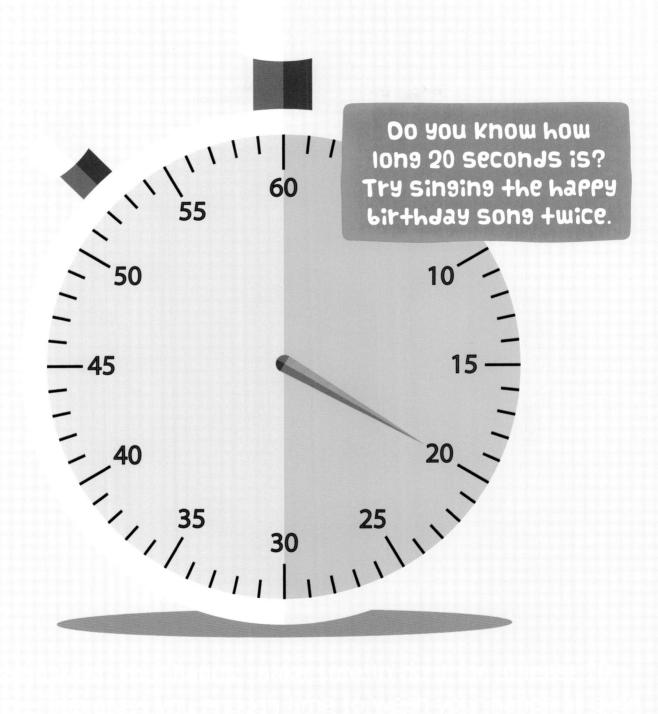

When Should You

Wash Your Hands?

Here are some times when you should wash your hands. Don't forget to use soap! Always wash your hands before:

Eating

Touching a cut, a scrape or a scratch

Touching your face

Always wash your hands after:

Going to the bathroom

Touching animals

Being outside

Playing in the park

Touching rubbish

Coughing or sneezing

Being near someone who is ill

15

How to Wash Your Hands

We can help stop germs and illnesses from spreading by washing our hands with soap and water. It is important to wash our hands properly.

3. Rub the backs of both hands.

2. Rub both palms together.

1. Wet hands with water and get lots of soap.

6.

Clean underneath each fingernail.

5.

Rub around each thumb.

4.

Rub in between all the fingers.

9.

Dry hands with a clean paper towel. Use the paper towel to turn off the tap.

8.

Rinse hands with water.

7.

Don't forget to rub around the wrists.

Healthy

There are other things you can do to keep your hands happy and clean.

Washing your hands can make them dry and sore.

Make sure you always dry them properly and use moisturiser after.

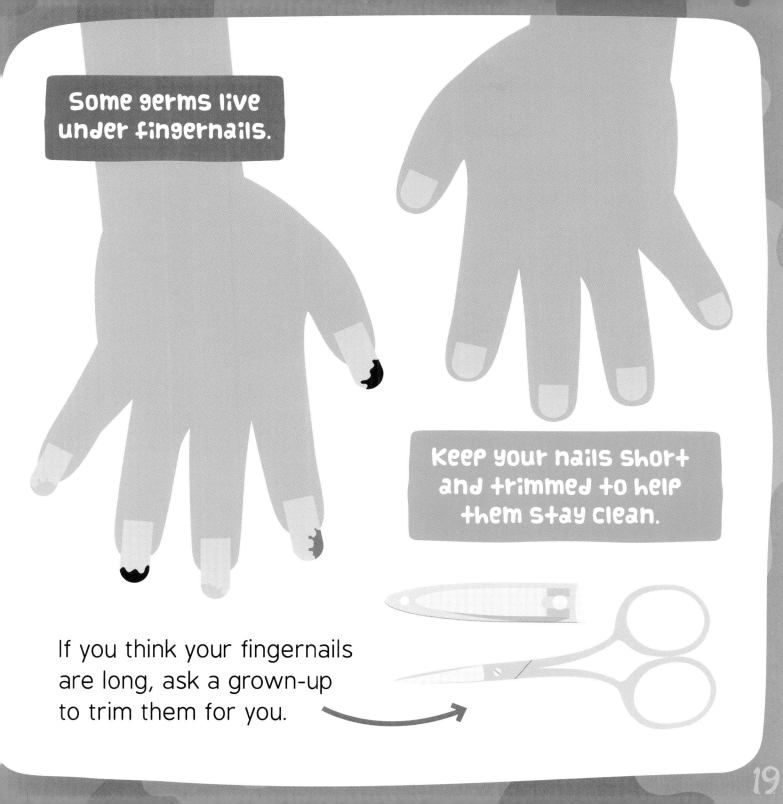

Some germs live under fingernails.

Keep your nails short and trimmed to help them stay clean.

If you think your fingernails are long, ask a grown-up to trim them for you.

What Else Can You Do?

Washing your hands can help you and other people stay safe from getting ill. Here are some other ways you can help.

Cover your mouth with a tissue when you cough or sneeze to stop the germs from spreading farther through the air.

After sneezing, make sure you put the tissue in the bin and wash your hands.

It's always better to wash your hands with soapy water if you can.

Hand sanitiser is a **gel** you can use to wash your hands when there is no soap or water nearby.

Squirt a little bit into your palm and rub it all over your hands, nails and wrists.

Germy

Some germs can live on your hands for a few hours if you don't wash them.

Your hands can carry millions of germs on them.

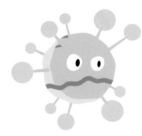

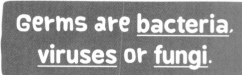
Germs are <u>bacteria</u>, <u>viruses</u> or <u>fungi</u>.

Activity

Look at these children. Should they wash their hands before or after what they are doing?

A.

B.

C.

D.

Answers: A. After, B. Before, C. After, D. Before

23

Glossary

bacteria   tiny living things, too small to see, that can cause diseases

fungi   living things that break down other living or dead things for food – mushroom, yeast and mould are all fungi

gel   something that looks like jelly

germs   tiny living things, too small to see, that can make people ill

moisturiser   a cream that makes your skin soft and smooth

surfaces   the outside or top layer of things

viruses   tiny living things, too small to see, that live inside other things and make them ill

Index